I0163710

How to Be a Prime Target

We're all targets
Some make better targets than others

Tom Peers

Ragamuffin Publishing © 2018

How to be a Prime Target

We're all targets
Some make better targets than others

Copyright © 2018 by Tom Peers

All rights reserved. No part of this publication may be reproduced, stored in a retrieval system, or transmitted in any form by any means-electronic, mechanical, photocopying, recording, or otherwise-without the prior written permission of the publisher.

Ragamuffin Publishing Company - Portland, Maine
tompeers53@gmail.com

How to be a Prime Target/ Tom Peers –

First edition

ISBN 13: 978-0-9970998-5-0

Unless otherwise marked, all Scripture quotations are taken from the English Standard Version (ESV).

Scripture marked "NLT" is taken from The Holy Bible, New Living Translation.

Scripture marked "NIV" is taken from The Holy Bible, New International Version.

Scripture marked "BBE" is taken from the 1949/1964 BIBLE IN BASIC ENGLISH.

Scripture marked "CEV" are from the Contemporary English Version.

Scripture from "GWT" is taken from God's Word Translation.

Printed in the United States of America

Watch out for your great enemy, the devil. He prowls around like a roaring lion, looking for someone to devour.

1 Peter 5:8
New Living Translation

Contents

Introduction

"The desire for safety stands against every great and noble enterprise."

- Tacitus (Roman historian, 56-120 AD)

"The desire for safety." All of us have an innate desire for safety and security. Only the insane disregard it. The good news is that God promises protection and safety to those who follow Him. The exception to this is persecution for being Christ-followers.

John 15:20

A servant is not greater than his master.' If they persecuted me, they will also persecute you.

But barring persecution, God's will is for His children to live blessed lives with divine protection, health/healing, provision, and many other blessings.

Psalm 91
1   He who dwells in the shelter of the Most High will abide in the shadow of the Almighty.
2   I will say to the Lord, "My refuge and my fortress, my God, in whom I trust."

1

3   For he will deliver you from the snare of the fowler and from the deadly pestilence.

4   He will cover you with his pinions, and under his wings you will find refuge; his faithfulness is a shield and buckler.

5   You will not fear the terror of the night, nor the arrow that flies by day,

6   nor the pestilence that stalks in darkness, nor the destruction that wastes at noonday.

7   A thousand may fall at your side, ten thousand at your right hand, but it will not come near you.

8   You will only look with your eyes and see the recompense of the wicked.

9   Because you have made the Lord your dwelling place—the Most High, who is my refuge—

10 no evil shall be allowed to befall you, no plague come near your tent.

11 For he will command his angels concerning you to guard you in all your ways.

12 On their hands they will bear you up, lest you strike your foot against a stone.

13 You will tread on the lion and the adder; the young lion and the serpent you will trample underfoot.

14 "Because he holds fast to me in love, I will deliver him; I will protect him, because he knows my name.

15 When he calls to me, I will answer him; I will be with him in trouble; I will rescue him and honor him.

16 With long life I will satisfy him and show him my salvation."

Why would God say this if He didn't want His children to live safe from the attacks of the enemy, spiritual or natural? The truth is, as long as there is a devil, there will be attacks. But there are steps we can take to mitigate the success of those attacks, and that is what this book is about. We will look at three characteristics of those who are prime targets.

I am omitting one characteristic of being a prime target because it should be an obvious assumption to Christians who are even partially familiar with the teachings of Scripture—that characteristic being living in sin. Notice I didn't say 'sin' but 'living in sin.' We all sin, probably daily, but living in sin is a different thing altogether. Living in sin is the habitual conscious practice of sin without genuine repentance.

1 John 3:4, 8-9

Everyone who makes a practice of sinning also **practices** lawlessness; sin is lawlessness. ... Whoever **makes a practice of** sinning is of the devil, for the devil has been sinning from the beginning. No one born of God **makes a practice of sinning**, for God's seed abides in him; and he cannot keep on sinning, because he has been born of God.

It could not mean that the simple act of sinning indicates a person is not born again because the Apostle John also said:

1 John 1:8

> If we say we have no sin, we deceive ourselves, and the truth is not in us.

So, it's not sin, but the PRACTICE of sin that would make someone a prime target.

Psalm 119:67

> Before I was afflicted I went astray, but now I obey your word.

Psalm 66:18

> If I had cherished iniquity in my heart, the Lord would not have listened.

Apart from intentionally living in known sin, there are three major characteristics that make someone a prime candidate for attack. Each deserves it own chapter, but first, we must open our eyes to the reality of a very real enemy who is bent on destroying us.

Chapter 1

We Have an Enemy

It's easy living in a natural/material world to forget that simultaneously we're living in a very real spiritual realm with God and Satan, along with angels and evil spirits. To the 21st-Century mind this seems fanciful, unreal, illogical, the thing that sci-fi movies are made of. The "fi" of "sci-fi" stands for *fiction*. To most, the idea of a realm other than the physical one is fiction.

All of our lives we've been well schooled in *scientism*. Science is good, scientism is bad. What is scientism? It's the philosophy that only the things that can be empirically verified by science using the scientific method are real and true. For something to be true using the scientific method it must meet two conditions—be observable and repeatable. A supernatural God and angels don't qualify, neither does a supernatural devil and his army of demons. Consequently, to most of us, if we can't see it or measure it with a scientific instrument, it's not real and true.

The Bible tells us about a man who didn't comprehend the spiritual realm, at least at first. He was the servant of a prophet by the name of Elisha. The backstory is about Israel's enemy, the king of Aram and the army of the Arameans, who sought to destroy Israel. Every time the Arameans would make plans to fight against the Israelites, the prophet Elisha would receive supernatural revelation from God about the impending attack and tell the king of Israel. The king of Israel would then instruct his army to flee whichever city the enemy army was marching towards. As you can imagine, this infuriated the king of Aram, who was convinced he had a traitor in the ranks.

2 Kings 6:11-12

> The king of Aram became very upset over this. He called his officers together and demanded, "Which of you is the traitor? Who has been informing the king of Israel of my plans?" "It's not us, my lord the king," one of the officers replied. "Elisha, the prophet in Israel, tells the king of Israel even the words you speak in the privacy of your bedroom!"

I'm so glad a prophet of God doesn't tell anyone the words I speak in the privacy of my bedroom, but that's a different story. Anyway, there was one time when God chose NOT to reveal to Elisha the plans of the Arameans, and he and his servant woke up surrounded.

2 Kings 6:15

> When the servant of the man of God got up early the next morning and went outside, there were troops, horses, and chariots everywhere.

"Oh, sir, what will we do now?" the young man cried to Elisha.

His natural fear wasn't unjustified, but the prophet Elisha was unfazed.

2 Kings 6:16-17

"Don't be afraid!" Elisha told him. "For there are more on our side than on theirs!" Then Elisha prayed, "**O Lord, open his eyes and let him see!**" The Lord opened the young man's eyes, and when he looked up, he saw that the hillside around Elisha was filled with horses and chariots of fire.

"Open his eyes and let him see!" When Elisha and his servant looked past the physical world into the spiritual realm, they saw a new reality...a myriad of God's angels on horses and chariots surrounding them ready to wage war against Israel's enemy. The young servant was oblivious to what was obvious to Elisha.

And so it is today, we have two kinds of people when it comes to an awareness of the spiritual realm, the *oblivious* and the *obvious*. Most are oblivious to the fact that there is a spiritual realm with a very real spiritual enemy. But to some who have studied these things and experienced spiritual oppression and warfare, it is obvious.

My goal is to help oblivious become obvious. It starts with two things:

1. Understanding that we're at war; and—
2. Understanding the enemy's tactics.

Only by correctly applying an understanding of these two things can we "fight the good fight of faith," and win (1 Timothy 6:12).

The problem is that, living in a physical world, we just focus on the physical. Our focus is on the wrong realm. For those Christ-followers who desire more spiritual victories, this needs to change. It requires looking at things with a new set of eyes.

2 Corinthians 4:18

As we look not to the things that are seen but to the things that are unseen. For the things that are seen are transient, but the things that are unseen are eternal.

At first blush this seems ridiculous. How can one look at things unseen? It's possible, but only with spiritual eyes. It is only then that we become aware of both our real enemy and the power of God available to us to experience victory in this life.

When World War I broke out, the War Ministry in London dispatched a coded message to one of the British outposts in the inaccessible areas of Africa. The message read: "War declared. Arrest all enemy aliens in your district." The War Ministry received back a prompt reply: "Have arrested ten Germans, six Belgians, four Frenchmen, two

Italians, three Austrians, and an American. Please advise immediately who we're at war with."[1]

This describes the conundrum for many Christians—they know they're at war, they can feel the oppression, attacks and heaviness every day, but they are oblivious who the real enemy is. But there's no need to be ignorant about this, Scripture makes clear who our real enemy is.

Ephesians 6:11-12

> Put on all of God's armor so that you will be able to stand firm against all strategies of the devil. For we are not fighting against flesh-and-blood enemies, but against evil rulers and authorities of the unseen world, against mighty powers in this dark world, and against evil spirits in the heavenly places.

2 Corinthians 10:3-4

> For though we live in the world, we do not wage war as the world does. The weapons we fight with are not the weapons of the world. On the contrary, they have divine power to demolish strongholds. (NIV)

Our battle is against evil spiritual principalities and powers, not against human beings. But most of us fight the wrong things. We are like the bull in the

---

[1] John Wimber, *The Way In is the Way On*, Ampelon Publishing, Pg. 139.

bullfight. The bull's real enemy is not the red cape but the person behind it. Corrie Ten Boom (*The Hiding Place*) said, "The first step to victory is to recognize the enemy."[2] Once recognizing our enemy, we must then recognize his strategy.

I love airplanes. I've always loved airplanes. That's why I'm a private pilot. One thing I love doing is going to airshows. I try to see one every summer. I guess because I served in the U.S. Air Force, I'm partial to the U.S. Air Force Thunderbirds, although I never miss seeing the Navy's Blue Angels either. I remember one time at an airshow watching the diamond formation (four F-16s grouped tightly together in a diamond) fly by us and then climb sharply away. And while our gaze was fixed on that diamond formation off in the distance, unseen by us, a Thunderbird F-16 came screaming from behind us at low altitude at a speed just shy of supersonic. We all jumped out of our skin. I heard people gasp, some screamed, babies cried, undergarments were soiled, and defibrillators were opened and on standby. Then the Thunderbirds narrator, over the sound system in that professional narrator voice said, "That, my friends, is what we call tactical surprise!"

It's nothing new in warfare. The strategy is to distract one's focus onto something secondary while the real problem lies elsewhere unseen. That's

---

[2] "Corrie Ten Boom." BrainyQuote.com. Xplore Inc, 2017. 24 July 2017.
https://www.brainyquote.com/quotes/quotes/c/corrietenb381182.html

exactly what the devil does. He distracts us with "the worries of this life, the lure of wealth, and the desire for other things." (Mark 4:19) And while we're distracted, Satan hits us from another direction.

From womb to tomb we're living in a warzone. There's no way around this, and Jesus knew it.

Matthew 10:16

> Behold, I am sending you out as sheep in the midst of wolves, so be wise as serpents and innocent as doves.

What kind of shepherd sends his sheep into a pack of wolves? But Jesus knew the reality of the world His followers were living in and wanted to prepare them spiritually and emotionally for the battle ahead. My point here is that we must understand that we have a spiritual enemy and then understand his tactics. Jesus filled us in on Satan's goals.

John 10:10

> The thief's purpose is to **steal** and **kill** and **destroy**.

Only when we understand who our real enemy is can we take intelligent and decisive action to overcome him. But make no mistake, a real spiritual enemy is looking to destroy God's people and His creation. He wants to destroy our:

- Happiness
- Marriage
- Children
- Body
- Finances
- Mind and emotions (happiness, peace)
- Future
- Career
- Time
- Holiness
- Relationships
- Community contribution
- Emotions
- Walk with God
- Reputation
- Peace of mind

Although human beings are oblivious, although they are asleep, Satan is not. He is very much on the loose 24/7, bent on stealing, killing, and destroying. He is actively looking for targets.

1 Peter 5:8

Stay alert! Watch out for your great enemy, the devil. He prowls around like a roaring lion, **looking for someone to devour.**

Satan and evil spirits roam around looking for someone to devour. They're looking for prime targets. And the truth is:

> We're all targets, but some people
> make better targets than others.

Christians who have their armor on and shield of faith up don't make the best targets. But others do.

I have one vivid memory from the first Iraq war in 1991, the Gulf War, also known as Operation Desert Storm. Many of us watched this war live on TV. We added to our vocabulary during this war...*scuds*. It all started when Saddam Hussein brazenly invaded the sovereign country of Kuwait. The insanity of thinking that goes into the decision to just go into another country to take over and seize its assets baffles my mind. Russia took the same action in the Ukrainian province of Crimea in 2014. Just invade and take over. But back to Iraq.

We saw oil fields burn as the Iraqi military began to high-tail it back to Baghdad, enacting their scorched earth philosophy. Long story short, as we kicked the Iraqi forces out of Kuwait, there was an extraordinarily long line of Iraqi tanks, trucks, jeeps, and armored personnel carriers on the way back to Iraq on "Highway 80," which came to be known as the "Highway of Death."[3] On February 26-27, 1991, our Air Force, Marine and Navy jet fighters

---

[3] https://en.wikipedia.org/wiki/Highway_of_Death

systematically picked off these vehicles one-by-one (or more like ten-by-ten). I've heard testimonies from the pilots who said there were so many jets waiting to bomb this long convoy that they had to fly circles high in the sky for hours (and refuel) just to get their turn to go in and unload their missiles and bombs. The retreating Iraqi forces were sitting ducks. They were in fact...prime targets.

There are similarites between this convoy and some Christians. That's what this book is about. And just to be clear, WE DON'T WANT TO BE PRIME TARGETS! We must do the exact opposite of the characterics mentioned in this book.

Additionally, we must understand that the devil, although our primary enemy, is not our only enemy.

Ephesians 2:1-3

> And you were dead in the trespasses and sins in which you once walked, following the course of this **world**, following **the prince of the power of the air**, the spirit that is now at work in the sons of disobedience—among whom we all once lived in the passions of **our flesh**, carrying out the desires of the body and the mind, and were by nature children of wrath, like the rest of mankind.

This passage identifies our three-fold enemy:
    1. The world.
    2. The flesh.
    3. The devil.

The World

Here we're not talking about the physical world or the people therein, people whom God loves dearly. By "world" we mean the evil and worldly order of things, the evil and anti-godly aspects of culture that, like Homer's sirens in his *Odyssey*, constantly sing to us their seducing songs hoping to take us in and eventually lead us to our own destruction. An evil and antichrist culture is like a Venus flytrap, visually attractive to pull the unsuspecting fly in, but once in, it's got it, no letting go.

James 4:4

Do you not know that **friendship with the world** is enmity with God? Therefore whoever wishes to be a friend of the world makes himself an enemy of God.

The answer is to resist the siren's call by allowing the Holy Spirit to transform us.

Romans 12:2

Do not be conformed to this world, but be transformed by the renewal of your mind, that by testing you may discern what is the will of God, what is good and acceptable and perfect.

The Flesh

"The flesh" is NOT our bodies. Excluding involuntary physical infirmities (like epilepsy), your body cannot do anything without permission from your mind. I've never involuntarily had a second helping of cake. My mind gave my hands permission to do that. The term "the flesh" in Scripture means that part of our soul (mind, will, intellect, thoughts and emotions) that is NOT transformed by the Holy Spirit or aligned in harmony with God and His Word. That part of our being that still struggles with temptation and sin the Bible calls "the old man" or "the old self."

2 Corinthians 5:17

Therefore, if anyone is in Christ, he is a new creation. The old has passed away; behold, the new has come.

The old has "passed away." But look at what the Apostle Paul said in another place.

Ephesians 4:22

Put off **your old self**, which belongs to your former manner of life and is corrupt through deceitful desires,

Why would we be told to put off something that's not there according to 2 Corinthians 5:17?

Colossians 3:9-10

> Do not lie to one another, seeing that you have
> put off **the old self** (your old sinful nature – NLT)
> with its practices and have put on **the new self**,
> which is being renewed in knowledge after the
> image of its creator.

You don't have to put or shake off something
that doesn't exist. The mere fact that we're
instructed to put off the old self or sinful nature
shows that it's still there and we struggle with it. *The
old self* is that part of us not conformed yet to God
and His Word. And as we can see from the verse, the
secret to putting on the new self is being renewed in
the knowledge of God, which is the Word of God.
God's Word, through the power of the Holy Spirit,
transforms us.

Psalm 119:11

> I have stored up your word in my heart, that I
> might not sin against you.

Hebrews 4:12

> For the word of God is alive and active. (NIV)

Therefore, "the flesh" is that part which still
struggles with sin. It's our own personal proclivities
and responses to evil. Evil is in the world pulling at
us and the part within us that is tempted by that evil

and even gravitates and responds to it is called "the flesh."

The Devil

The devil is an actual person. He is not a fuzzy ambiguous evil force. Just as Jesus is a real person, so is the devil. Just as angels are real beings, so are evil spirits (demons).

Matthew 4:1-3, 5-11

¹ Then Jesus was led up by the Spirit into the wilderness to be tempted by the devil.

² And after fasting forty days and forty nights, he was hungry.

³ And the tempter came and said to him...

⁵⁻⁶ Then the devil took him to the holy city and set him on the pinnacle of the temple and said to him...

⁸⁻⁹ Again, the devil took him to a very high mountain and showed him all the kingdoms of the world and their glory. And he said to him...

¹¹ Then the devil left him.

The devil was a real person who spoke real words to Jesus. He tempted Jesus with words, he temped Adam and Eve with words (Genesis 3), but he generally won't speak to you or me audibly like that. With you and me he tempts with the siren's song of allurement to do evil and be "conformed to this world" (Romans 12:2). It's not quite as overt as with Jesus and Adam and Eve.

So we have the world, the flesh and the devil. But behind all evil is this very real spiritual enemy, the devil. Behind the evil of *the world* and *the flesh* is a spiritual power. The devil is the one who is behind the world's system of business, entertainment, fashion, education, science, politics, military, art and commerce.

> "Behind all that is tangible we meet something intangible, we meet a planned system; and in this system there is a harmonious function, a perfect order."
>
> - Watchman Nee, Love Not the World[4]

For the most part, even Christians are unaware of the spirit behind these realms. There will come a time in the new earth under the reign of Christ that all things will be godly, but not now. There is a spiritual mad dog that is bent on influencing all of these areas to his own end—to lure humanity to renounce God and His ways. There's a reason the devil has these titles or said to have power.

---

[4] Watchman Nee, Love Not World, CLC Publications, 2004

2 Corinthians 4:3-4	the god of this world
John 14:30	the ruler of the world
John 12:31	the ruler of this world
Ephesians 2:2	the prince of the power of the air
1 John 5:19	the whole world lies in the power of the evil one

All but two of these verses were said AFTER the resurrection of Christ! So we are dealing with a very real enemy bent on our destruction. He doesn't play fair, he doesn't play nice, his goal is to steal, kill and destroy (John 10:10).

The devil *prowls around like a roaring lion, looking for someone to devour.* We're all targets, but some make better targets than others. So, what does he look for? What makes someone a prime target? Let's find out.

Chapter 2

Characteristic 1 - Unsuspecting

So, what makes someone a prime target? We'll use Judges 18 as our anchor passage to find out. In this passage, we see three distinguishing characteristics of being a prime target.

Judges 18 is about the tribe of Dan looking for land to settle in. As the Israelites crossed over the Jordan River and into the land of Canaan, they conquered territories and eventually assigned land to the various tribes of Israel. This chapter is the story of the tribe of Dan looking for suitable land and once finding it, its effort to conquer the inhabitants.

They eventually decided to invade the town of Laish. Laish was a town in the very north of Israel (or Canaan back then), near the border of Syria. After the tribe of Dan defeated it, Laish was renamed to *Dan*, and is known as *Tel Dan* today.[5] A "tel" is a hill or mound caused by the destruction of an ancient city. They would destroy a city and then rebuilt another on top of it, gradually creating a hill with streets, homes and buildings above the old ruins. But why did the Danites (people of the tribe of Dan) decide to invade Laish? We see in Judges 18

---

[5] https://en.wikipedia.org/wiki/Dan_(ancient_city)

that Laish was ripe for invasion because it possessed three key characteristics which made them prime targets. In this chapter we'll deal with the first one.

Judges 18:1-2, 7-10, 27-28

1   Now in those days Israel had no king. And the tribe of Dan was trying to find a place where they could settle, for they had not yet moved into the land assigned to them when the land was divided among the tribes of Israel.

2   So the men of Dan chose from their clans five capable warriors from the towns of Zorah and Eshtaol to scout out a land for them to settle in.

7   So the five men went on to the town of Laish, where they noticed the **people living carefree lives,** like the Sidonians; they were **peaceful and secure (quiet and unsuspecting –** ESV). The people were also wealthy because their land was very fertile (their land lacked nothing – NIV). And they lived a great distance from Sidon and had no allies nearby.

8   When the men returned to Zorah and Eshtaol, their relatives asked them, "What did you find?"

9   The men replied, "Come on, let's attack them! We have seen the land, and it is very good.

What are you waiting for? Don't hesitate to go and take possession of it.

¹⁰ When you get there, you will find the people living **carefree lives**. God has given us a spacious and fertile land, lacking in nothing!"

²⁷ Then, with Micah's idols and his priest, the men of Dan came to the town of Laish, **whose people were peaceful and secure**. They attacked with swords and burned the town to the ground.

²⁸ There was no one to rescue the people, for they lived a great distance from Sidon and had no allies nearby. This happened in the valley near Beth-rehob. Then the people of the tribe of Dan rebuilt the town and lived there. (NLT)

Verse 7   Carefree, peaceful, secure, quiet, unsuspecting
Verse 10   Carefree lives
Verse 27   Peaceful and secure

In the South they have a saying, they'd call this "fat, dumb and happy." In other words, not a care in the world.

Safe, Secure, Carefree & Unsuspecting

The first characteristic of a prime target is that they feel safe, secure, carefree and are unsuspecting. The connection should be obvious, when you feel safe and secure you drift toward become carefree and unsuspecting. In other words, when you feel safe and secure, you're not looking around, you're not keeping your guard up, you're not watching for an enemy attack, you're just tooling along "fat, dumb, and happy." And that is the perfect time to be attacked. It is the danger of a peacetime army instead of an army maintaining a high degree of military readiness.

That defines the problem with most Christians— we're NOT a peacetime army, we're at war! But as stated earlier, most Christians are oblivious to the fact that we're at war, and so their "shield of faith" (Ephesians 6:16) is lowered, and when that happens, the enemy's arrows find their target.

In 1912, Jessie Penn-Lewis came out with a book called, *War on the Saints*. Her book became a classic as she opened the eyes of a sleepy Christendom to the reality of spiritual warfare against Satan and his army of evil spirits. Later she wrote, *The Warfare with Satan,* and other books dealing with spiritual warfare. More recently, Frank Peretti woke the church up with his series of novels, starting with *This Present Darkness* and later *Piercing the Darkness*. Although novels, they were based on Scripture and served to shock Christians into an awareness of the reality of Ephesians 6:12.

Ephesians 6:12

> For we are not fighting against flesh-and-blood enemies, but against evil rulers and **authorities of the unseen world**, against mighty powers in this dark world, and against evil spirits in the heavenly places.

Jesus taught that we have authority over the enemy and that we should be using it.

Luke 10:19

> Look, I have given you authority over all the power of the enemy, and you can walk among snakes and scorpions and crush them. Nothing will injure you.

"Snakes and scorpions" are metaphors here to mean Satan and his demons and by extension, wicked people. It's hard to use our authority to push back the enemy when we're not even aware we have an enemy or are at war in the first place.

What made the town of Laish ripe for attack was that they felt safe, secure, carefree and unsuspecting...totally unaware of a very real enemy about to attack them. The New Living Translation uses the words *carefree, peaceful and secure*, while the English Standard Version says *quiet and unsuspecting*.

Judges 18:7

So the five men went on to the town of Laish, where they noticed the **people living carefree lives,** like the Sidonians; they were **peaceful and secure (quiet and unsuspecting** – ESV). (NLT)

The Bible in Basic English (BBE) makes it even clearer:

"living without thought of danger."

This false sense of security resulted in the inhabitants of Laish "living carefree lives."

Jesus talked about a man who spent all his time, money and effort living a carefree life without any thought of what really mattered. It didn't end well.

Luke 12:16-21

16 Then he told them a story: "A rich man had a fertile farm that produced fine crops.

17 He said to himself, 'What should I do? I don't have room for all my crops.'

18 Then he said, 'I know! I'll tear down my barns and build bigger ones. Then I'll have room enough to store all my wheat and other goods.

¹⁹ And I'll sit back and say to myself, "My friend, you have enough stored away for years to come. **Now take it easy! Eat, drink, and be merry!**"

²⁰ "But God said to him, 'You fool! You will die this very night. Then who will get everything you worked for?'

²¹ "Yes, a person is a fool to store up earthly wealth but not have a rich relationship with God."

The unsuspecting, carefree life with a false sense of security doesn't end well. It causes us to focus on "lesser things," things not of primary importance.

I'm amazed, shocked actually, at how many people don't think about God or the afterlife. God and eternity are not even on their radar. In such cases I always think, "Really? You could unexpectantly die in a car accident or of a heart attack in the next six hours, and you haven't even taken the time to investigate the claims of Jesus Christ, heaven or how to get there? Really?" People put exponentially more time into planning their vacation and retirement than to their eternity. To me, that's the epitome of carefree and unsuspecting. Like the inhabitants of Laish, it doesn't end well.

I think one could legitimately make the case that, for the most part, our military at Pearl Harbor on December 6, 1941 felt safe, secure and was carefree and unsuspecting. The same could be said of the crew of the Titanic on April 14, 1912, the day before it sank. It could also be said of the upper management at NASA on January 28, 1986, the day of the space shuttle Challenger disaster. Safe, secure, carefree and unsuspecting doesn't end well. That's true in the natural realm as well as the spiritual.

The greatest danger to Christians is not overt sin, although that's becoming more and more of an issue. No, the greatest danger to Christians is apathy and spiritual complacency. It doesn't end well.

Proverbs 1:32

> For the simple are killed by their turning away, and **the complacency of fools destroys them.**

Complacency destroys! Instead of putting on their armor and raising their shields (Ephesians 6), people opt for their bathing suits and beach umbrellas. Safe, secure, carefree, unsuspecting. But that's a perfect setup for a sneak attack from the enemy. We must stay alert and vigilant.

Acts 20:29, 31

> Fierce wolves will come in among you, not sparing the flock ... Therefore be alert.

Vigilance and Prayer

The solution to the danger of a carefree and unsuspecting life is: 1) we must understand that we have an enemy seeking to destroy us, and 2) we must stay vigilant.

1 Peter 5:8

Stay alert! Watch out for your great enemy, the devil. He prowls around like a roaring lion, looking for someone to devour. (NLT)

The Contemporary English Version reads:

Be on your guard and stay awake.

The message is clear: When you have an enemy seeking to destroy you, stay alert! But how?

One of the main ways we keep spiritually alert is by regular and focused prayer.

Colossians 4:2

Never give up praying. And **when you pray, keep alert** and be thankful. (CEV)

Mark 14:38

Watch and pray that you may not enter into temptation.

Ephesians 6:18

> Pray in the Spirit at all times and on every occasion. **Stay alert and be persistent in your prayers** for all believers everywhere. (NLT)

Immediately before Ephesians 6:18 (*stay alert*) is the passage about putting on spiritual armor with the shield of faith. Why? Because we're in warfare! And the Apostle Paul culminates the spiritual warfare passage with a command to stay alert in prayer. The admonition to keep alert in prayer is because there's a natural tendency to daydream in prayer. This happens to me without exception. I'll start to pray and then my mind strays to thinking about all kinds of things not at all related to what I'm praying about. I don't think this is caused by the devil so much as it is the human condition. There's no doubt about it, focused vigilant prayer takes discipline.

What is the connection between vigilant prayer and not being a prime target? I believe Jesus gave us a clue in John 16.

John 16:14

> When the Spirit of truth comes, he will guide you into all the truth, for he will not speak on his own authority, but whatever he hears he will speak, **and he will declare to you the things that are to come.**

When in focused prayer, the Holy Spirit will show us things to come, including an impending enemy sneak attack, much the same as we saw with Elisha in 2 Kings 6:8-12. There are many times in prayer I've experience the whisper of the Holy Spirit about an impending enemy attack against me, a family member, a friend, our church, or even our nation. Why would the Holy Spirit reveal such a thing? The answer should be plain, so we'll pray and cut it off before it even happens! But...we have to have our prayer-radar sweeping the spiritual landscape and be paying attention to it.

The key to vigilant prayer is undistracted prayer. This is why Jesus stated:

Matthew 6:6

> But when you pray, go into your room and **shut the door** and pray to your Father who is in secret. And your Father who sees in secret will reward you.

"Shut the door" because you want to stay focused and eliminate distractions. Today Jesus would have said, "Go into your room, shut the door and turn off your smart phone and every other electronic device." This may seem crazy, but I even insert ear plugs to help me create an atmosphere of total silence.

The point is—the way we stay vigilant is in prayer. Put another way:

Non-praying people are targets!

Non-praying people are not even in a place where the Holy Spirit can whisper guidance to them. They are oblivious. I believe this is what the Spirit of God is saying to the church today: "Hey down there, wake up, be watchful and attentive, because there's a real devil and he's out to steal, kill and destroy, so you better stay alert." This is exactly what was said in 1 Peter 5:8: *Stay alert! Watch out for your great enemy, the devil.*

Characteristic 1 for being a prime target is: Just live life as usual, don't worry, be happy. You're not in danger. There's nothing to stay alert about, nothing could ever happen to you. Don't pray a hedge of protection around you, your family, or your church, there's no need. Relax!"

People who are carefree and have a false sense of security are prime targets. But knowing that you have an enemy waiting to attack and keeping vigilant are not the only critical issues here.

Familiarization with Our Weapons

The first step in preventing a sneak attack, as our previous chapter touched on, is to realize that we have a very real enemy out to destroy us. Secondly, we must keep vigilant in prayer. But there's one more critical element we must touch on.

The third step is to have an intimate familiarization with our spiritual weapons. However, here we have a two-fold problem: 1) most Christians don't even though they have these weapons and 2) even if they do, they don't have experiential knowledge of how to use them. The time to have an experiential or working knowledge of one's weapons is BEFORE the attack comes. And the weapons we are talking about here are not the worldly weapons of guns or bombs. No, our weapons are spiritual.

2 Corinthians 10:3-4

For though we walk in the flesh, we are not waging war according to the flesh. For the weapons of our warfare are not of the flesh but have divine power to destroy strongholds.

It doesn't say we don't have weapons, it says our weapons are not carnal, fleshly or what we would consider the normal weapons of this world. So, what are our spiritual weapons?

Weapons of our Warfare

We have a number of weapons at our disposal, I'll briefly mention four.

1. The Word of God

Ephesians 6:17

> The sword of the Spirit, which is the word of God

A sword is both an offensive and defensive weapon. We underestimate the power of speaking God's Word. Notice I didn't say reading and studying God's Word, I said speaking it. The devil knows God's Word too as you'll notice in the following passage, but Jesus spoke and declared God's Word in fighting off the devil's attacks.

Matthew 4:1-11

> 1 Then Jesus was led up by the Spirit into the wilderness to be tempted by the devil.
>
> 2 And after fasting forty days and forty nights, he was hungry.
>
> 3 And the tempter came and said to him, "If you are the Son of God, command these stones to become loaves of bread."

⁴ But he answered, **"It is written**, "'Man shall not live by bread alone, but by every word that comes from the mouth of God.'"

⁵ Then the devil took him to the holy city and set him on the pinnacle of the temple

⁶ and said to him, "If you are the Son of God, throw yourself down, for it is written, "'He will command his angels concerning you,' and "'On their hands they will bear you up, lest you strike your foot against a stone.'"

⁷ Jesus said to him, **"Again it is written**, 'You shall not put the Lord your God to the test.'"

⁸ Again, the devil took him to a very high mountain and showed him all the kingdoms of the world and their glory.

⁹ And he said to him, "All these I will give you, if you will fall down and worship me."

¹⁰ Then Jesus said to him, "Be gone, Satan! **For it is written**, "'You shall worship the Lord your God and him only shall you serve.'"

¹¹ Then the devil left him, and behold, angels came and were ministering to him.

Three temptations and three times they were conquered by speaking God's Word. This is the example left us if we want to be victorious over the attacks of the enemy. God's Word has power.

Jeremiah 23:29

> Is not my word like fire, declares the LORD, and like a hammer that breaks the rock in pieces?

When the Apostle John addressed young Christian men, he connected overcoming Satan with God's Word.

1 John 2:14

> I write to you, young men, because you are strong, and the word of God abides in you, and you have overcome the evil one.

Putting it all together, the Word of God must; 1) reside within us (through study, meditation and memorization) and 2) be spoken and declared in the midst of attack.

2. Prayer

Although we've already mentioned vigilance in prayer, it's worth repeating that prayer is a powerful weapon for believers.

Luke 22:46

> Why are you sleeping? Rise and pray that you may not enter into temptation.

There is an obvious connection between prayer and experiencing victory in the midst of temptation. Spiritual power and ability are experienced by those who turn to God and trust Him in prayer.

3. The name of Jesus

Here is a true but understated fact—there is power in the name of Jesus. He has been given the name above all names (Philippians 2:9). And we have been given this name to rule over and conquer the devil. After Jesus commissioned seventy disciples to go into every town and proclaim the gospel and heal the sick, the disciples came back and reported what happened.

Luke 10:17-19

> The seventy-two returned with joy, saying, "Lord, even the demons **are subject to us in your name!**" And he said to them, "I saw Satan fall like lightning from heaven. Behold, I have given you authority to tread on serpents and scorpions, and over all the power of the enemy, and nothing shall hurt you.

The point here…the devil and demons are subject to us in Jesus' name. The name of Jesus has power and authority. When the Apostle Paul was being harassed by a demon-possessed person, notice what he said.

Acts 16:18

Paul, having become greatly annoyed, turned and said to the spirit, "I command you **in the name of Jesus Christ** to come out of her." And it came out that very hour.

There is power in that name!

4. Praise & Worship.

Our motivation for praising and worshipping God is because He is worthy. At the same time, we must understand that, like prayer, when we engage in praise and worship, we begin to sense God's presence and power. That power is released to still the enemy.

Psalm 8:2

Through the praise of children and infants you have established a stronghold against your enemies, to silence the foe and the avenger. (NIV)

Notice in 2 Chronicles 20 what happens when the congregation of Israel worships God when faced with almost certain annihilation from the enemy.

2 Chronicles 20:18-23

18 Then Jehoshaphat bowed his head with his face to the ground, and all Judah and the

inhabitants of Jerusalem fell down before the Lord, worshiping the Lord.

19 And the Levites, of the Kohathites and the Korahites, stood up to praise the Lord, the God of Israel, with a very loud voice.

20 And they rose early in the morning and went out into the wilderness of Tekoa. And when they went out, Jehoshaphat stood and said, "Hear me, Judah and inhabitants of Jerusalem! Believe in the Lord your God, and you will be established; believe his prophets, and you will succeed."

21 And when he had taken counsel with the people, he appointed those who were to sing to the Lord and praise him in holy attire, as **they went before the army,** and say, "Give thanks to the Lord, for his steadfast love endures forever."

22 And when they began to sing and praise, the Lord set an ambush against the men of Ammon, Moab, and Mount Seir, who had come against Judah, so that they were routed.

23 For the men of Ammon and Moab rose against the inhabitants of Mount Seir, devoting them to destruction, and when they had made an end of the inhabitants of Seir, they all helped to destroy one another.

When faced with spiritual oppression or attack, spend time in praise and worship. More times than not I accomplish this by playing and singing along with worship music on my smart phone. I don't need worship music to worship God, but it enhances and energizes my worship all the more.

Our Armor

Although armor is not a weapon, it's defensive, it's worth mentioning here. Weapons are good, weapons with armor is better. When attacked, not only should we have an intimate familiarization with our weapons, but we should also put on the armor of God.

Ephesians 6:10-18

10 Finally, be strong in the Lord and in the strength of his might.

11 Put on the whole armor of God, that you may be able to stand against the schemes of the devil.

12 For we do not wrestle against flesh and blood, but against the rulers, against the authorities, against the cosmic powers over this present darkness, against the spiritual forces of evil in the heavenly places.

¹³ Therefore take up the whole armor of God, that you may be able to withstand in the evil day, and having done all, to stand firm.

¹⁴ Stand therefore, having fastened on the belt of truth, and having put on the breastplate of righteousness,

¹⁵ and, as shoes for your feet, having put on the readiness given by the gospel of peace.

¹⁶ In all circumstances take up the shield of faith, with which you can extinguish all the flaming darts of the evil one;

¹⁷ and take the helmet of salvation, and the sword of the Spirit, which is the word of God,

¹⁸ praying at all times in the Spirit, with all prayer and supplication.

It is essential to be wearing "the armor of God." It's called the armor of God because it is God-given. I believe it's more appropriate to say, "the armor from God." The Contemporary English Version says, "So put on all the armor that God gives." God's Word Translation renders it, "Take up all the armor that God supplies." What pieces of armor does the Lord supply us with to defend ourselves against the attacks of Satan?

1. The belt of truth.

John 17:17

> Sanctify them in the truth; your word is truth.

The belt of truth means knowing, acting on, and speaking God's Word. We saw this earlier in Matthew 4 when Jesus spoke the truths of God's Word every time He was attacked by Satan, "It is written."

2. The breastplate of righteousness.

"Righteousness" means "right-standing with God." When we accept Christ as our Lord and Savior, we are made righteous in God's sight. Our right-standing with God is not based on personal merit, but on God's grace through faith. Knowing that we are in right-standing with God protects us from fear, condemnation and sin-consciousness.

Romans 5:17

> Those who receive the abundance of grace and the free gift of righteousness reign in life through the one man Jesus Christ.

3. Feet that are ready and prepared to share the Good News of peace with God.

This requires **knowing** the Word of God in order to share the Word of God.

1 Peter 3:15

> Always being prepared to make a defense to anyone who asks you for a reason for the hope that is in you; yet do it with gentleness and respect.

4. The helmet of salvation.

Putting on the armor of God begins by receiving Jesus Christ and experiencing salvation. Helmets protect one's head (brain & mind). If we KNOW we are saved, that knowledge protects our thinking.

1 John 5:13

> I write these things to you who believe in the name of the Son of God, that you may KNOW that you have eternal life.

We can KNOW that we're saved, not wonder about it. When the devil, who is called "the accuser of the brethren" (Revelation 12:10) assaults us with thoughts of unworthiness, the helmet of salvation anchors our minds with hope.

Hebrews 6:19

> We have this hope as an anchor for the soul.

5. The sword of the Spirit, which is the Word of God.

Like a sword, the Word of God is both offensive and defensive. The weapon of the Spirit, in other words, the weapon that the Spirit uses to conquer our spiritual enemy, the devil, is God's Word. Even when Jesus returns, this is the primary weapon.

Revelation 1:16

> Coming out of his mouth was a sharp, double-edged sword.

Revelation 19:15

> From his mouth comes a sharp sword with which to strike down the nations.

We must be armed with the sword of the Spirit, which is the Word of God. This means we must know it and speak it when in spiritual warfare.

6. The shield of faith.

Take note especially of verse 16 which talks about our shield of faith, "In addition to all of these, hold up the shield of faith to stop the fiery arrows of the devil." We won't cover this now because I've devoted an entire chapter to it, Chapter 5.

To summarize

The first characteristic of being a prime target is to be unsuspecting, feeling safe, carefree and secure. To NOT be a prime target we must:

1. Understand that we have an enemy.

2. Understand the enemy's tactics (i.e. distraction).

3. Have our spiritual radar up (vigilant prayer).

4. Have an intimate experiential knowledge of our weapons.

5. Wear our spiritual armor.

Chapter 3

Characteristic 2 - Isolated

The first characteristic of a prime target is to feel safe, secure, carefree and unsuspecting. Here we're talking about a false sense of security at a time when a very real spiritual enemy is seeking a target to "kill, steal and destroy." Our anchor verse is from 1 Peter.

1 Peter 5:8

Stay alert! Watch out for your great enemy, the devil. He prowls around like a roaring lion, looking for someone to devour. (NLT)

The second characteristic of being a prime target is to be isolated. Isolation, not regularly connected to meaningful relationships, kills.

Have you ever seen video footage of a lion in Africa stalking a herd of gazelle? Is the lion's goal to eat the whole herd? No, it's goal is to go after one, and which one does the lion go after? It goes after the gazelle that gets broken off and isolated from the rest of the herd. The isolated gazelle is a prime target for a prowling lion.

In our passage from Judges 18, the town of Laish was isolated, which marked them as being a prime target.

Judges 18:7, 28

7   So the five men went on to the town of Laish, where they noticed the people living carefree lives, like the Sidonians; they were peaceful and secure (quiet and unsuspecting – ESV). The people were also wealthy because their land was very fertile (their land lacked nothing – NIV). **And they lived a great distance from Sidon and had no allies nearby.**

28   There was no one to rescue the people, for they lived a great distance from Sidon and had no allies nearby. (NLT)

The town of Laish was isolated and disconnected. They were loners, and consequently, when attacked, there was no one to offer them help. Scripture confirms the danger of isolation.

Ecclesiastes 4:9-10

Two people are better off than one, for they can help each other succeed. If one person falls, the other can reach out and help. But **someone who falls alone is in real trouble.** (NLT)

It's interesting that in 1991, during the Gulf War, not one nation came to Iraq's side. This made for an easy defeat. Who does the lion go after? The lone gazelle. Who do cults go after? Do cults go after huge crowds during crusades? No, they go after the person sitting on a park bench all alone.

Spiritually, this shows the importance of being connected to other believers in meaningful relationships. I must add, not just connected, but closely connected. It shows the importance of being in a good, Bible-believing local church and coming under the oversight of a good pastor and elders.

Hebrew 13:17

> Obey your leaders and submit to them, **for they are keeping watch over your souls**, as those who will have to give an account. Let them do this with joy and not with groaning, for that would be of no advantage to you.

Pastors and elders "keep watch over your soul." That speaks of protection, protection that is only afforded to us when we meet regularly with other believers.

Hebrews 10:24-25

> And let us consider how to stir up one another to love and good works, **not neglecting to meet together**, as is the habit of some, but

encouraging one another, and all the more as you see the Day drawing near.

I would also add that is also means meeting in a weekly small group of some type, whether that's in a classroom, home, or coffee shop. The weekly larger celebration service on the weekend at church is needed, but so is meeting with a small group of people during the week.

Acts 2:46

And day by day, attending **the temple** together and breaking bread **in their homes**, they received their food with glad and generous hearts.

Acts 5:42

And every day, in **the temple** and **from house to house**, they did not cease teaching and preaching that the Christ is Jesus.

Acts 20:20

How I did not shrink from declaring to you anything that was profitable, and teaching you **in public** and **from house to house**.

This means having a small cadre of Christians in your life that you are tightly knit to. By regularly participating in the larger church celebration on weekends plus a small group during the week, believers protect themselves and secure the support of others.

Why People Isolate

I will admit something to you, I have a natural drift towards isolation. We all tend to drift toward our personal preferences. "Tom, are you implying that you prefer isolation over community?" No, I don't want to imply that at all—I want to flat out state that. If I had the choice between staying home reading or chilling out or going to church or a small group meeting, I'd choose to stay home every single time (unless it was donut Sunday). I really can't explain this but the older I get, the more I move from the extrovert to the introvert side of the continuum. If I'm home with my wife and puppy, curled up with my tablet device reading a book, watching a sermon or aviation video on YouTube, or watching a movie, I'm happier than a mosquito at a nudist colony. But…the closer I get to God the more I realize I must fight this personal preference and discipline myself to engage in community. I personally attend the weekly Sunday service as well as a mid-week small group. I do it because I want to please God, and I know it's healthy for me. Otherwise, I become susceptible to becoming a prime target. But it takes personal discipline to do this. So why is it that people isolate?

Why People Isolate

1. **They simply don't see the need or benefit.**
   - When they do a cost-benefit analysis, they think that the cost of community outweighs the benefits. Ultimately, we make time for what's important.

2. **They are too busy.**
   - They have overloaded their calendar without creating margin in their lives.

3. **They are natural introverts.**
   - They are more energized by being alone than with people.

4. **They've been "burned" in the past.**
   - Sometime in the past they've been double-crossed or hurt by someone. To that I say, "Join the club, grow up and get over it."

5. **They don't like accountability.**
   - They may be observed and subsequently called into account and corrected on their beliefs or behavior. This is the fear of being known. Someone may discover they're not perfect and have an issue or two.

6. **They're experiencing interpersonal conflict.**
   - There's someone at church or small group they have a conflict with. It's just easier to stay

home than resolve the conflict through the Matthew 18:15-17 process.

7. They have experienced tragedy or loss.

- With some people, tragedy or the loss of a loved one causes them to withdraw. In Genesis 37, Joseph's brothers reported to their father, Jacob, that Joseph had been killed. This wasn't true, but that's what they told Jacob. Verse 35 says, *All his sons and all his daughters rose up to comfort him, **but he refused to be comforted.*** It is possible to refuse to be comforted, even after a normal and adequate period of time of grieving. At that point grief become pathological (a sickness). People experiencing significant tragedy and loss need to be nurtured back to health and reengage in community.

Like me, many people, for whatever reason, naturally drift toward isolation. But that natural drift must be resisted and measures taken to counteract it. Isolation makes one a prime target.

Regarding #1 above, *They simply don't see the need or benefit*, it might help to see the benefits of being in community.

Benefits of Community

By "community" we mean regularly attending a good, biblically based church as well as a small group led by mature believers. There are numerous benefits to moving out of isolation and into community.

1. It models the Godhead.

Deuteronomy 6:4

> Hear, O Israel: The LORD our God, the LORD is one.

But God is also a trinity.

Matthew 3:16-17

> And when Jesus was baptized, immediately he went up from the water, and behold, the heavens were opened to him, and he saw the Spirit of God descending like a dove and coming to rest on him; and behold, a voice from heaven said, "This is my beloved Son, with whom I am well pleased."

Our God is one, yet, God is a trinity; Father, Son and Holy Spirit. The mere fact that God in the trinity is a community shows the importance of His will for His people, for we are made in His image (Genesis 1:27).

Acts 2:41-42

[41] So those who received his word were baptized, and there were added that day about three thousand souls.

[42] And they devoted themselves to the apostles' teaching and the fellowship, to the breaking of bread and the prayers.

The New Testament knows nothing of isolation and individualism. Acts 12 tells the story of Peter being put in prison by Herod. Herod's full intention was to execute Peter (verses 1-3). But notice verse 5.

Acts 12:5

So Peter was kept in prison, but earnest prayer for him was made to God **by the church.**

Peter was prayed for by others who knew about his predicament. But that's the key...they have to know about it! How many people have needs that are never shared with other believers because they isolate, or, even if with other Christians, never share their needs for prayer and support? As a result of the Christian community's prayers, Peter experienced a miraculous deliverance from prison. An Angel awakened Peter and escorted Peter out of prison. It was so astounding that Peter wasn't even sure it was real. And the first thing Peter did when released from prison was to go back to the very people he was in community with, the same people who prayed for him.

Acts 12:11-12

> When Peter came to himself, he said, "Now I am sure that the Lord has sent his angel and rescued me from the hand of Herod and from all that the Jewish people were expecting." When he realized this, he went to the house of Mary, the mother of John whose other name was Mark, where many were gathered together and were praying.

Again, this shows the New Testament pattern for believers.

5. Accountability.

One of the benefits of being in community and not isolation is accountability. For some, accountability is the very reason they DON'T engage in community. They have a natural aversion to accountability. I think we all do. But accountability is the thing that helps us grow spiritually. Every one of us have a need for others to gracefully speak into our lives and challenge us to keep in community along with growing spiritually. If we isolate we take ourselves out of the environment of community where accountability takes place. Some will quip, "Oh, but I have that kind of accountability with my spouse." I don't believe that. Maybe I don't believe that because I know it's not true in my own life. It's all too easy to blow off the encouragement, admonition or correction of a spouse. We are more apt to take it to heart when it comes from others spoken in love.

Ephesians 4:15

> Speaking the truth in love, we are to grow up in every way into him who is the head, into Christ,

And when we hear truth spoken in love, we have a choice; we can either ignore it or take it to heart.

Ephesians 5:21

> Submitting to one another out of reverence for Christ.

Are we ready to allow others to speak into our lives? The reality of these scriptural admonitions can only realistically take place in community as opposed to isolation.

6. Protection.

Earlier in this chapter we quoted Hebrews 13:17 which speaks of pastors and church leaders watching over our souls because they are accountable to God for us. This is God's way of protecting His sheep. We see thing again in Acts 20, where the Apostle Paul warns the church leaders from the city of Ephesus about wolves coming in and harming the sheep.

Acts 20:28-31

> Pay careful attention to yourselves and to all the flock, in which the Holy Spirit has made you overseers, to care for the church of God, which he obtained with his own blood. I know that after my departure fierce wolves will come in among you, not sparing the flock; and from among your own selves will arise men speaking twisted things, to draw away the disciples after them. Therefore be alert.

The church leaders here were tasked with protecting the sheep from wolves. But...what if a sheep decides to isolate and not stay part of the flock? The answer is obvious, it becomes a prime target.

7. Spiritual growth and change.

Growth requires change. However, spiritual growth is team sport, not a solo sport. The problem is that most people have the typical and highly American "It's a private thing between me and God" attitude. One of the benefits of community is that is allows others to help in our spiritual growth and change.

Ephesians 4:16

> He makes the whole body fit together perfectly.
> As each part does its own special work, it helps
> the other parts grow, so that the whole body is
> healthy and growing and full of love. (NLT)

Notice here the connection between growth and the contribution of others. When we come together, each part contributes and helps the other parts grow.

Proverbs 27:17

> As iron sharpens iron, so one person sharpens
> another. (NLT)

Community helps its members sharpen one another. This simply can't happen in isolation.

8. Corrects bad theology.

Being in community, both in the larger church and small group contexts, allows our theology (views about God) to be shaped in healthy ways. It also serves as a safeguard against doctrinal error. Whether from sermons from the pulpit or with a small group of believers studying scripture in a home, errant beliefs can be politely challenged and corrected. This might be why some people don't appreciate community...they don't want their pet beliefs challenged. Today I hold certain theological views that were errant but were corrected when someone challenged those views.

2 Timothy 2:25

> Gently instruct those who oppose the truth. Perhaps God will change those people's hearts, and they will learn the truth.

In Acts 18, a convert to Christianity by the name of Apollos because to preach and spread the gospel. But Apollos needed some adjusting on his theology. Thank God he received it.

Acts 18:24-26

> Now a Jew named Apollos, a native of Alexandria, came to Ephesus. He was an eloquent man, competent in the Scriptures. He had been instructed in the way of the Lord. And being fervent in spirit, he spoke and taught accurately the things concerning Jesus, though he knew only the baptism of John. He began to speak boldly in the synagogue, but when Priscilla and Aquila heard him, **they took him aside and explained to him the way of God more accurately.**

As accurate as we think we are, there is someone who can help us become even more accurate.

9. Helps to identify your spiritual gifts.

There are spiritual gifts, and we should be using them.

1 Corinthians 12:1

> Now concerning spiritual gifts, brothers, I do not want you to be uninformed.

1 Peter 4:10

> Each of you should use whatever gift you have received to serve others, as faithful stewards of God's grace in its various forms

We discover our spiritual gifts in a number of ways, one of which is when others see gifts in us and affirm them. I give more credence to others identifying and affirming our gifts then to a survey we fill out. We can fudge on the survey, but we can't fudge (for too long) when others observe us. Being in regular community affords people the opportunity to help identify our spiritual gifts.

10. Becomes the context of receiving care and nurture.

1 Corinthians 12:25

> That there may be no division in the body, but that the members may have the same care for one another.

Being connected in the body of Christ will result in its members caring for one another. But care cannot happen if one chooses to isolate from the body. This care and nurture comes in the form of encouragement, counsel, hospitality, prayer, and sometimes even financial or material support. The Book of Acts has a beautiful picture of this.

Acts 2:44-45

> And all who believed **were together** and had all things in common. And they were selling their possessions and belongings and distributing the proceeds to all, as any had need.

Notice these key words "were together." Needs can only be known and met when those in need are together with others in the faith community. I cannot encourage and pray for you unless we interact together and you are transparent enough to disclose what's going on in your life. We'll never know or be able to support loners who isolate and aren't transparent about their needs and challenges.

11. Serves in evangelism.

The local church and small group become places to invite spiritual seekers so that they can hear and be exposed to the gospel of Jesus Christ, the presence of God and His people. The most effective evangelism strategy is one which partners individual believers with the local church. Very few people are able to do it all; share Christ with others, pray for people to become born again, and help disciple them in spiritual growth. But when church attenders become "inviters," spiritual seekers can attend church with them and respond to an invitation (altar call) to receive Christ. Additionally, there are some small groups that are totally geared toward reaching people for Christ, the Alpha program being one of these.[7] Those isolated can't avail themselves to the partnering with the local church in evangelism.

12. Increases the joy factor in our spiritual journey.

Choosing community over isolation increases our joy factor as we are on this journey of spiritual growth. When I was in the Air Force stationed near Adana, Turkey, I took a military hop over to Athens, Greece for a few days. After that I took another hop over to Tel Aviv, Israel and met a friend with whom I backpacked around Israel for a week or so. But I was in Athens by myself for about four days. So here I am in Athens, walking around the Acropolis and Parthenon all by myself, and guess what? Instead of it being a blast, my joy tank was only a quarter full because there was no one with me to enjoy the experience. As soon as I met my friend Dave in Israel, the joy tank got filled up. When the Apostle Paul was in prison and isolated he wrote to Timothy:

---

[7] https://alphausa.org/about/

2 Timothy 1:4

I long to see you, that I may be filled with joy.

Being alone...terrible. Being with someone else you know well brings joy. In the same chapter Paul talks more about experiencing isolation and its remedy.

2 Timothy 1:15-18

You are aware that all who are in Asia turned away from me, among whom are Phygelus and Hermogenes. May the Lord grant mercy to the household of Onesiphorus, **for he often refreshed me** and was not ashamed of my chains, but when he arrived in Rome **he searched for me earnestly and found me**— may the Lord grant him to find mercy from the Lord on that day!—and you well know all the service he rendered at Ephesus.

Paul was isolated in prison and everyone turned away from him, but a visit by Onesiphorus refreshed him. Life is better when we travel together.

13. Where we learn to resolve relational conflict.

One of the biggest indicators of spiritual and emotional growth is how we resolve relational conflict. Jesus gave us instruction on how this works.

Matthew 18:15-17

> If your brother sins against you, go and tell him his fault, between you and him alone. If he listens to you, you have gained your brother. But if he does not listen, take one or two others along with you, that every charge may be established by the evidence of two or three witnesses. If he refuses to listen to them, tell it to the church. And if he refuses to listen even to the church, let him be to you as a Gentile and a tax collector.

One can't grow in the skill of resolving conflict if isolated. We learn this skill best when in community with others who love us and who know biblical principles of conflict resolution.

14. Models community to the next generation.

Children learn from their parents, and not so much *taught* as *caught*. God blessed Abraham because He knew Abraham would model godliness to the next generation.

Genesis 18:19

> For I have chosen him, **that he may command his children and his household after him to keep the way of the LORD** by doing righteousness

> and justice, so that the LORD may bring to Abraham what he has promised him.

When kids see their parents isolating and not engaged in community, they will emulate that. Conversely, when our children see their parents regularly involved in church on weekends and in a small group during the week, they will learn the value of being members in the Body of Christ.

15. Expands our thinking to new ideas and perspectives.

Because we're human, we tend to become myopic (tunnel vision) with our own views, ideas and perspectives in life. But by engaging regularly in community we expand our views of both Scripture and life. Our thinking opens up to other views about all sorts of issues. This is a good thing. But when we stubbornly hold onto our own opinions without being open to others, we short circuit growth and become susceptible to becoming a prime target.

Proverbs 18:1-2, 13

> Whoever isolates himself seeks his own desire; he breaks out against all sound judgment. A fool takes no pleasure in understanding, but only in expressing his opinion. ... If one gives an answer before he hears, it is his folly and shame.

Our judgment in life is sharpened when dialoging with others.

16. Becomes a witness to a disconnected world.

Engaging in regular community also models and becomes a witness to our extended families, co-workers, neighbors and friends, many of whom are isolated and lonely and inwardly yearn for community. The Beatles song *Elinor Rigby* says, "All the lonely people, where do they all come from? All lonely people, where do they all belong?" The answer...they're everywhere and from every place. Where do they belong? Connected in community, not isolated. One way to change this is to not hide the fact that we're going to church and attending a weekly small group. And when unchurched people see the members of the Body of Christ caring for one another, they will take notice. Acts 2 shows the impact upon others that this kind of love and care produced.

Acts 2:44-47

And **all who believed were together** and had all things in common. And they were selling their possessions and belongings and **distributing the proceeds to all, as any had need.** And day by day, attending the temple together and breaking bread in their homes, they received their food with glad and generous hearts, praising God and **having favor with all the** people. And the Lord added to their number day by day those who were being saved.

17. The place where we can express our gifts.

This is different from #9 above - *Helps to identify your spiritual gifts.* This point is about the context for, not identifying, but expressing our spiritual gifts. Spiritual gifts are not for ourselves, but for the benefit of others.

1 Corinthians 12:4-7

Now there are varieties of gifts, but the same Spirit; and there are varieties of service, but the same Lord; and there are varieties of activities, but it is the same God who empowers them all in everyone. To each is given the manifestation of the Spirit **for the common good.**

If our gifts are for the common good, then it requires us to engage and participate in regular community. Someone with the leadership gift requires followers. Someone with the teaching gift requires learners. Someone with the gift of mercy requires people to show mercy to. You get the idea. Community gives us a venue, a context to express our spiritual gifts. Verse 21 however, shows the mindset of isolation.

1 Corinthians 12:21

> The eye cannot say to the hand, "I have no need
> of you," nor again the head to the feet, "I have
> no need of you."

"No need of you" = isolation.

18. It creates and builds friendships.

It should be obvious that participating in regular community results in creating and building friendships. Americans are funny, we yearn for connectedness but won't do what it takes to get it. There is no worse feeling than that expressed by David in Psalm 142 when he was hiding in a cave.

Psalm 142:4

> Look to the right and see: there is none who
> takes notice of me; no refuge remains to me; no
> one cares for my soul.

Unfortunately, that is the sentiment of many people. They suffer in muted pain. But when experiencing genuine community, life changes, the journey becomes one of joy.

Proverbs 17:17

> A friend loves at all times, and a brother is born
> for adversity.

The key is to build friendships with the right kind of people, people who you enjoy being around. And realistically...you will only have a half dozen or less of these kinds of friends. So you must have your radar up and be seeking friends that will be a good fit. We call it "the gel factor." These people just seem to gel with your type of personality, humor and worldview.

There are three kinds of people:

1. Energizers
- If you're at a party with energizers you don't want the party to end.

2. Drainers
- When you're at a party with drainers you're looking for an excuse to leave.

3. Neutrals
- If at a party with neutrals, you won't even know they were there. "They were at the party?"

Find the energizers, find those who you can't wait to get around. Even though I naturally gravitate toward isolation, I make a concerted effort to engage in community. It takes work, but it's worth it. And here is the brutal truth about isolation versus community:

Isolation:
>Feels better in the short term but is detrimental in the long term.

Community:
>Is very hard short term but pays big dividends long term.

One of the marks of the last days is that believers will separate themselves from the faith (and church).

1 Timothy 4:1

>Now the Spirit expressly says that in later times some will **depart from** the faith (NIV - **abandon** the faith) by devoting themselves to deceitful spirits and teachings of demons.

You can't depart from or abandon something you weren't first part of. This shows the people in question here are believers. Thayer's Greek Lexicon says that this word "depart" or "abandon" means, "to stand aloof."[8] Therefore, the last days will be marked by Christians "standing aloof" from church and the faith. When a believer breaks off from the pack and stands aloof, they are prime targets.

From Judges 18, the city of Laish was a prime target because they were isolated.

---

[8]   https://www.blueletterbible.org/lang/lexicon/lexicon.cfm?Strongs=G868&t=KJV

Judges 18:

    7   And they lived a great distance from Sidon and had no allies nearby.

    28   There was no one to rescue the people, for they lived a great distance from Sidon and had no allies nearby. (NLT)

How to be a prime target?
1. Unsuspecting (safe, secure, carefree).
2. Isolated.

Our next chapter focuses on our last characteristic, one that may cause angst in some readers.

Chapter 4

Characteristic 3 - Wealthy

This will make those who are wealthy (or those who want to be) recoil somewhat, but hear me out on this. It is certainly possible for wealthy people to live fully devoted lives to Jesus Christ, I know plenty of them. However, wealth DOES present a significant challenge to undistracted commitment in following Christ. Jesus said so.

Mark 10:23

> How difficult it will be for those who have wealth to enter the kingdom of God!

Although it doesn't have to be, wealth and prosperity can be a perfect setup to becoming a prime target.

In our anchor passage from Judges 18, we see the tribe of Dan searching for a city to invade so they can capture the land for their own possession. After sending spies into the area to scout out the possibilities, they came to the city of Laish. Here in Judges 18 we find out that Laish was a prime target for attack. Keying in on our third characteristic of being a prime target, we again look at the passage.

Judges 18:1-2, 7

¹ Now in those days Israel had no king. And the tribe of Dan was trying to find a place where they could settle, for they had not yet moved into the land assigned to them when the land was divided among the tribes of Israel.

² So the men of Dan chose from their clans five capable warriors from the towns of Zorah and Eshtaol to scout out a land for them to settle in.

⁷ So the five men went on to the town of Laish, where they noticed the people living carefree lives, like the Sidonians; they were peaceful and secure (quiet and unsuspecting – ESV). **The people were also wealthy because their land was very fertile (their land lacked nothing – NIV).** And they lived a great distance from Sidon and had no allies nearby.

⁸ When the men returned to Zorah and Eshtaol, their relatives asked them, "What did you find?"

⁹ The men replied, "Come on, let's attack them! We have seen the land, and it is very good. What are you waiting for? Don't hesitate to go and take possession of it.

¹⁰ When you get there, you will find the people living carefree lives. God has given us a **spacious and fertile land, lacking in nothing!"**

²⁷ Then, with Micah's idols and his priest, the men of Dan came to the town of Laish, whose people were peaceful and secure. They attacked with swords and burned the town to the ground.

²⁸ There was no one to rescue the people, for they lived a great distance from Sidon and had no allies nearby. This happened in the valley near Beth-rehob. Then the people of the tribe of Dan rebuilt the town and lived there. (NLT)

Verse 7 The people were also wealthy because their land was very fertile (their land lacked nothing – NIV)

Verse 10 You will find the people living carefree lives. God has given us a spacious and fertile land, lacking in nothing!

We can see here another reason for Laish being a prime target. Not only were they unsuspecting and isolated, they were wealthy, which added to the danger. I'll explain.

The problem with wealth is three-fold:
1. It adds to a false sense of security.
2. It fosters independence from God.

3. It distracts to secondaries which produces lukewarmness.

1. Wealth and a False Sense of Security

We covered in detail the trap of a false sense of security in Chapters 1 and 2, but we'll mention it again as it relates to wealth.

When one is wealthy there is the tendency, even though subconscious, for that wealth to make one feel safe and secure. The wealthy can live in protective, gated communities. They can drive the best cars, send their children to the best schools, buy the best healthcare, have a savings account that will last them until they're a hundred years old, buy the best jet and hire the best pilots...on and on. But all of this contributes to a false sense of security, especially when it comes to their relationship with God and eternity.

Wealthy people fail to recognize four things:

1. They'll never think they have enough.

Ecclesiastes 5:10

Whoever loves money never has enough; whoever loves wealth is never satisfied with their income. (NIV)

Ecclesiastes 6:9

> Enjoy what you have rather than desiring what you don't have. Just dreaming about nice things is meaningless—like chasing the wind. (NLT)

The biblical answer for this never-ending quest for more is contentment.

1 Timothy 6:8

> But if we have food and clothing, with these we will be content.

2. Wealth can't give peace or happiness long term.

It can't buy marital and family harmony. Many times wealth brings pain and destruction.

1 Timothy 6:9

> But those who desire to be rich fall into temptation, into a snare, into many senseless and harmful desires that **plunge people into ruin and destruction.**

All one needs to do is make a list of actors, musicians and sports heroes who have taken their own lives to realize this. Money is a great servant but a terrible master.

3. Wealth is fleeting.

James 4:14

You do not know what tomorrow will bring.

Proverbs 23:5

In the blink of an eye wealth disappears, for it will sprout wings and fly away like an eagle. (NLT)

James 1:9-11

Let the lowly brother boast in his exaltation, and **the rich in his humiliation**, because like a flower of the grass he will pass away. For the sun rises with its scorching heat and withers the grass; its flower falls, and its beauty perishes. **So also will the rich man fade away in the midst of his pursuits.**

4. Wealth can't buy health.

Apple founder Steve Jobs is just one of a myriad of examples of this. Jamaican musician Bob Marley's last words to his son were, "Money can't buy you life."[9] He died at the age of thirty-six from cancer.

---

[9] https://en.wikipedia.org/wiki/Bob_Marley

I referenced this passage in Chapter 2, but it bears repeating. Jesus told a story one time that drives this point home—wealth results in a false sense of security.

Luke 12:13-21

13 Someone in the crowd said to him, "Teacher, tell my brother to divide the inheritance with me."

14 But he said to him, "Man, who made me a judge or arbitrator over you?"

15 And he said to them, "Take care, and be on your guard against all covetousness, for one's life does not consist in the abundance of his possessions."

16 And he told them a parable, saying, "The land of a rich man produced plentifully,

17 and he thought to himself, 'What shall I do, for I have nowhere to store my crops?'

18 And he said, 'I will do this: I will tear down my barns and build larger ones, and there I will store all my grain and my goods.

19 And I will say to my soul, "Soul, you have ample goods laid up for many years; relax, eat, drink, be merry."'

> 20 But God said to him, 'Fool! This night your soul is required of you, and the things you have prepared, whose will they be?'
>
> 21 So is the one who lays up treasure for himself and is not rich toward God."

Verse 19 shows the man's attitude: "You have it made, relax, don't worry...be happy." The man in this story had a false sense of security caused by his wealth. He didn't realize that it all burns up in the end. As they say, "I've never seen a hearse pulling a U-Haul." The man didn't have an eternal perspective because Jesus said in verse 21 that he "was not rich toward God." But Jesus taught a whole different perspective on wealth, one with a focus on eternity.

Matthew 6:19-21

> Do not lay up for yourselves treasures on earth, where moth and rust destroy and where thieves break in and steal, but lay up for yourselves treasures in heaven, where neither moth nor rust destroys and where thieves do not break in and steal. For where your treasure is, there your heart will be also.

2. Fosters Independence From God

Not only does wealth add to a false sense of security, but it also creates an attitude of self-sufficiency and independence from God. It's a failure to understand that all things come "from above, coming down from the Father of lights." (James 1:17) Even the ability you have to make wealth doesn't come from you, but from God!

Deuteronomy 8:18

> You shall remember the Lord your God, for it is he who gives you power (ability) to get wealth, that he may confirm his covenant that he swore to your fathers, as it is this day.

It's God that gives us creativity, intellect, skill, business acumen and entrepreneurial savvy. God wants us to place our trust in Him and nothing else. Whatever we're trusting in besides God is an idol. For some, wealth is an idol that usurps God's rightful place as the most important thing in one's life. Anything that becomes an idol will ultimately be our downfall.

Proverbs 11:28

> Whoever trusts in his riches will fall, but the righteous will flourish like a green leaf.

It's not a sin to be wealthy, but it is a sin to put one's hope in riches instead of God.

1 Timothy 6:17

> As for the rich in this present age, charge them not to be haughty, **nor to set their hopes on the**

uncertainty of riches, but on God, who richly provides us with everything to enjoy.

Jeremiah 2:13

My people have committed two evils: they have forsaken me, the fountain of living waters, and hewed out cisterns for themselves, broken cisterns that can hold no water.

The people talked about here were God's people for God said, "My people." They should have known better but they didn't. They had a two-fold sin. First, they forgot God, their source. The Jews had been warned about this before.

Deuteronomy 6:10-12

And when the Lord your God brings you into the land that he swore to your fathers, to Abraham, to Isaac, and to Jacob, to give you—with great and good cities that you did not build, and houses full of all good things that you did not fill, and cisterns that you did not dig, and vineyards and olive trees that you did not plant—and when you eat and are full, **then take care lest you forget the Lord**, who brought you out of the land of Egypt, out of the house of slavery.

Did this happen to the Jews? Yes.

Hosea 13:4-6

> But I am the Lord your God from the land of Egypt; you know no God but me, and besides me there is no savior. It was I who knew you in the wilderness, in the land of drought; but when they had grazed, **they became full, they were filled, and their heart was lifted up; therefore they forgot me.**

Forgetting God was their first sin. Their second sin was creating systems of wealth and provision totally disconnected from God, systems that were self-made and dependent on their own human accomplishments: *hewed out cisterns for themselves, broken cisterns that can hold no water.* I'm sure they were very proud of everything they built, but they found out that what they had built by their own human efforts didn't work. Their efforts were futile.

Proverbs 23:4

> Do not wear yourself out to get rich; do not trust your own cleverness. (NIV)

Notice the self-sufficiency, "do not trust your own cleverness." Smart people, wealthy people seem to trust their own abilities instead of God. Eventually they find out it doesn't work. This is problem #2 of wealth...it fosters independence from God.

3. Distracts and Causes Lukewarmness

The first problem with wealth is that it gives a false sense of security. The second is that it fosters an attitude of independence from God. The third problem with wealth is that it distracts and pulls us away from the main thing (following Christ) and subsequently results in lukewarmness.

When I was pastoring in Rochester, New York, there was a couple who started coming to our church. They had just gone through bankruptcy. They were without a good job. But they accepted Christ and kept learning about God, prayer, and faith. They attended regularly and started tithing and God started to really change things around for them financially. Pretty soon they were able to buy a great house. Then a little later, as they continued to be blessed, they bought a camper-trailer. And then, slowly, you didn't see them as much anymore. Pretty soon you didn't see them at all. It was a case of Deuteronomy 6:10-12, "then take care lest you forget the Lord." I can repeat that story over and over with people that bought boats and cottages and got into new hobbies and forms of recreation.

Is there anything inherently wrong with boats, cottages, camping RVs or trailers? Not at all. The problem occurs when these things acquired from wealth distract and pull us away from God, His kingdom and His body (the body of Christ, the church).

85

Jesus warned about this. In the parable of the sower and seed, seed represents the word of God. Some seed fell among thorns which choked out the seed so that it never produced (Mark 4:7). When the disciples asked Jesus what this meant, Jesus explained this aspect of the parable to them.

Mark 4:18-19

> And others are the ones sown among thorns. They are those who hear the word, but **the cares of the world** and **the deceitfulness of riches** and **the desires for other things** enter in and choke the word, and it proves unfruitful.

Jesus identified three things that distract and pull us away from full devotion to Him:
1. The cares of this world.
2. The deceitfulness of riches.
3. The desires for other things.

"Why can't you go to small group?" "Well, that's the night we …" "I haven't seen you at church in a while." "Well, that's because we're at the cabin on weekends." On and on it goes. What has happened? All three have happened; the cares of this world, the deceitfulness of riches, and the desires for other things." There is the real tendency for wealth to draw us away to these three things. The issue here is priorities…first things first.

Matthew 6:33

> But seek **first** the kingdom of God and his righteousness, and all these things **will be added to you.**

Notice the word "added." Jesus doesn't mind things being added to us. God's nature is to add to us, not subtract. But the condition is IF we put Him and the kingdom of God first. If our wealth is not connected to intense and full commitment to Christ, we become lukewarm. Notice what Jesus said to the church at Laodicea in the book of Revelation.

Revelation 3:14-18

14 And to the angel of the church in Laodicea write: "The words of the Amen, the faithful and true witness, the beginning of God's creation.

15 I know your works: you are neither cold nor hot. Would that you were either cold or hot!

16 So, because **you are lukewarm,** and neither hot nor cold, I will spit you out of my mouth.

17 For you say, I am rich, I have prospered, and I need nothing, not realizing that you are wretched, pitiable, poor, blind, and naked.

18 I counsel you to buy from me gold refined by fire, **so that you may be rich,** and white

garments so that you may clothe yourself and the shame of your nakedness may not be seen, and salve to anoint your eyes, so that you may see."

This passage in Revelation 3 describes a church full of people who became lukewarm because of their wealth. "I am rich, I have prospered, and I need nothing" sounds like the people in the city of Laish in Judges 18:7, *lacking nothing that is in the earth and possessing wealth.* The problem wasn't that they had wealth, the problem was that wealth had them!

Wealth and prosperity lead to lukewarmness towards God and the things of God if they are not coupled with intense, full commitment in following Christ. That is the natural human trajectory of wealth if not checked by spiritual discipline.

Wealth hindering one's spiritual journey is so prevalent that Jesus openly declared the magnitude of the problem.

Mark 10:23, 25

How difficult it will be for those who have wealth to enter the kingdom of God!" ... It is easier for a camel to go through the eye of a needle than for a rich person to enter the kingdom of God.

The disciples were shocked at Jesus' statement.

Mark 10:26

> And they were exceedingly astonished, and said to him, "Then who can be saved?"

But Jesus assures them that it IS possible to have wealth and still be fully devoted to Him.

Mark 10:27

> Jesus looked at them and said, "With man it is impossible, but not with God. For all things are possible with God."

According to Jesus, having wealth and fully following Christ is not impossible, it's just that it's very difficult. Those are the words of Jesus, not mine. Untethered to full and radical devotion to following Christ, wealth sets people up to become prime targets.

This probably sounds like I'm making the case that God's people shouldn't be wealthy, but that is not true. When I look at scripture I see over and over that God's will is to bless His people with ample provision, barring those times of lack or poverty due to persecution for being Christ-followers. Let me explain.

Is Abundance God's Will?

I don't believe it's God's will for His people to live in poverty or lack. Like I said, the only exception I see to this unfortunate circumstance is during times of persecution for being believers in Christ or possibly voluntary poverty to reach a certain people-group. We are not redeemed from persecution and there will times when ungodly oppressors force Christ-followers into lack and poverty. A look at the Apostle Paul's life shows that he experienced lack and pressing circumstances quite a bit, all due to his preaching of the gospel. But apart from that, I believe Scripture is clear that God wants to meet our needs and even go beyond that so that we experience abundance (and I will qualify that shortly).

I love asking groups of people this question: Is God's will that we live:
- without our needs being met?
- our needs just barely being met?
- that we live in a sane, measured degree of abundance?

Many times I'll whiteboard this out by drawing three different horizontal lines depicting the three choices.

1. Abundance _____

2. Needs being met _____

3. Needs NOT being met _____

I'll ask, "Barring times of persecution or voluntary poverty to reach a people-group, which line does God want His children to live on?" By far, most people who answer this devious setup question answer line #2, needs just being met. But this is not true, and here are two reasons why. First, scriptural support, and second, logic. If we are to be givers (and we are), then one can't give what one doesn't have (although there are times we'll give beyond our ability and means, see 2 Corinthians 8:3)! Generous giving requires abundance, a level that exceeds our needs barely being met.

For example, John the Baptist instructed those who had two coats to give to the one who had none (Luke 3:11). But if we don't have an extra coat we can't do that!

If we're reprimanded for asking for things from God, it's because we're asking with wrong motives...for our own worldly passions and desires.

James 4:2-4

> You do not have, because you do not ask. **You ask and do not receive, because you ask wrongly, to spend it on your passions.** You adulterous people! Do you not know that friendship with the world is enmity with God?

The NIV states it this way:
James 4:3

> When you ask, you do not receive, because you ask with wrong motives, that you may spend what you get on your pleasures. (NIV)

Asking for things just to satisfy one's carnal pleasures is equated with adultery! Why? Adultery is when someone transfers their love, devotion and loyalty to someone else whom they are not united with. And who, according to James 4, do we transfer those things to? We transfer them from Christ to the world and worldly thinking. There's a difference between praying for a nice car that is adequate and that will last a long time and praying for a Porsche 911 ($100,000). The problem is not with us having things, it's with things having us! Even if one is a billionaire, I would argue that one should use restraint and purchase for practical need, not to impress or flaunt, actions which are the antithesis of Christlikeness. One can purchase a $100,000 car, but I would argue scripturally, it's not beneficial or constructive to the virtues of humility that Christ modeled for us. Paul touched on this.

1 Corinthians 10:23

> "I have the right to do anything," you say—but not everything is beneficial. "I have the right to do anything"—but not everything is constructive. (NIV)

When we answer the question, "Is God's will for His people abundance," we must define *abundance*. It simply means more than needed, excess. It's pictured in Psalm 23:5, "You anoint my head with oil; my cup **overflows**."

Socio-Culturally Defined

Abundance is socio-culturally defined. If a person lives in the United States and works fifteen miles away, only owning a bicycle would not be abundance. If this same person had no savings account and lived paycheck to paycheck, this also would not be abundance. it would be line #2 above, with just your needs being met with none to spare. But let's take a very poor city in a third world country where everyone has to walk a sizeable distance to work, but this person has a bicycle— that's abundance. The person who lives on a mountain in Ecuador where just having your needs met meant owning six chickens, but this person owned nine, that's abundance. So we must be careful to view abundance in light of our current social and cultural realities.

Abundance is defined by:
1. Age
2. Country
3. Education
4. Occupation
5. Family financial history
6. Income level

The definition of abundance to a person working in a low end fast-food restaurant is quite different from a CEO of a fortune 500 business. The person in the low-end job who had $5,000 in savings would be thrilled. The CEO would be gripped with fear. But in either case, the real question is, is abundance God's will?

Abundance is God's Will

I don't teach that God's will for His people is *wealth* (as far as we normally define it), but I do teach that *abundance* is God's will. This may seem totally contrary to the very essence of this chapter, but I am obligated as a teacher to present truth in (hopefully) a balanced way. So, is abundance for God's children biblical? As we survey the New Testament, we see God will as an ever-emerging pattern.

John 10:10

The thief comes only to steal and kill and destroy. I came that they may have life and have it **abundantly**.

John 21:4-6

Just as day was breaking, Jesus stood on the shore; yet the disciples did not know that it was Jesus. Jesus said to them, "Children, do you have any fish?" They answered him, "No." He said to them, "Cast the net on the right side of the boat, and you will find some." So they cast it, and now they were not able to haul it in, **because of the quantity of fish**.

Matthew 25:29

To those who use well what they are given, even more will be given, and **they will have an abundance**. (NLT)

Luke 6:38

Give, and it will be given to you. Good measure, pressed down, shaken together, **running over**, will be put into your lap.

Matthew 14:20

And they all ate and were satisfied. And they took up **twelve baskets full of the broken pieces left over**.

Philippians 4:18

> I have received full payment **and have more than enough**. I am amply supplied. (NIV)

2 Corinthians 9:8

> And God will generously provide all you need. Then you will always have everything you need and **plenty left over** to share with others. (NLT)

2 Corinthians 8:9

> For you know the grace of our Lord Jesus Christ, that though he was rich, yet for your sake he became poor, so **that you by his poverty might become rich**.

Let me mention two things about this verse. First, some people try to spiritualize this verse by saying this is talking about spiritually, not materially. They fail to take the verse in context because chapters eight and nine of 2 Corinthians is talking about material giving and receiving. Besides that, looking at the verse, Jesus became poor spiritually? I don't think so. Jesus, in comparison to what He had before coming down to earth to live as a man, became poor. He said, "Foxes have holes, and birds of the air have nests, but the Son of Man has nowhere to lay his head." (Luke 9:58) This is NOT talking about spiritually. Second, it's easy to take the word "rich" here to mean something it doesn't. It simply means to have an abundance. It is the

Greek word "plouteō" and literally means, "to have an abundance" or "to be richly supplied."[10] If we define "rich" as having expensive cars, owning a 10,000 square foot home, owning a yacht and vacation home on the ocean, we have it all wrong. That is NOT how scripture defines the word. It means abundance, being richly supplied, and…to have an abundance and be richly supplied is, as we have shown, is God's will.

I have purposely tried to stick to the New Testament for this point, but it is worth noting that in the Old Testament, poverty was not God's will and was in fact, part of the curse from Deuteronomy. Deuteronomy 28:15

> But if you will not obey the voice of the Lord your God or be careful to do all his commandments and his statutes that I command you today, then all these curses shall come upon you and overtake you.

Reading down from verse 15 we see that poverty is one of the preeminent curses mentioned numerous times in one form or another. Poverty and lack is not God's will. But provision and abundance IS God's will.

---

[10] https://www.blueletterbible.org/lang/lexicon/lexicon.cfm?Strongs=G4147&t=KJV

Deuteronomy 30:9

> The Lord your **God will make you abundantly prosperous in all the work of your hand,** in the fruit of your womb and in the fruit of your cattle and in the fruit of your ground. For **the Lord will again take delight in prospering you,** as he took delight in your fathers.

Psalm 34:10

> Those who seek the Lord **lack no good thing.**

One fly in the ointment here is the problem of prosperity teachers who teach an extreme version of this message of abundance. These teachers err in two ways; both in the degree of abundance they advocate and the frequency in how much they preach it. There is such a thing as "error by overemphasis." I also would add that they err by their own lifestyles, which exceed "excellence" and step into "extravagance." Excellence is good, extravagance—not so good.

In touching on the subject of abundance, I'd like to give you three reasons why this is God's will for us.

Three Reasons for Abundance

There are three main reasons that God's will for His children is to live in abundance, just not barely getting their needs met.

1.   To finance the gospel.

The main reason God wants us to live in abundance is connected to His main mission, the spread of the gospel. Again, you cannot give what you do not have.

> "God prospers me not to raise my standard of living, but to raise my standard of giving."
> - Randy Alcorn [11]

I can't count the number of times in a church service that I wanted to take the checkbook and write out a check for $1,000 to some missionary who was speaking, or some Christian benevolence organization being represented, but couldn't...I didn't have it. The main reason for God blessing us is to use us as channels to finance the spread of the gospel.

Deuteronomy 8:18

> You shall remember the LORD your God, for it is he who gives you power to get wealth, that he may confirm his covenant that he swore to your fathers, as it is this day.

---

[11] Randy Alcorn, The Treasure Principle, 2005, p. 75, Multnomah Books

Genesis 12:2

> And I will make of you (Abraham) a great nation, and I will bless you and make your name great, so that you will be a blessing.

God said to Abraham, "I'm going to bless you SO THAT you will be a blessing." The primary reason we're blessed is not for ourselves, but for others, in the case of Abraham, to bless the nations (verse 3 - *in you all the families of the earth shall be blessed*). Abraham being used of God to bless the nations of the whole earth was about getting His Word and covenant out to the world. The more we are blessed financially the more we tithe and give offerings.

2.   To give to those in need.

The second reason God wants us to live in abundance and be richly supplied is to meet the needs of others.

2 Corinthians 9:8

> And God will generously provide all you need. Then you will always have everything you need and plenty left over to share with others. (NLT)

Ephesians 4:28

> Let him labor, doing honest work with his own hands, so that he may have something to share with anyone in need.

Again, you can't give what you don't have. "Let him who has two coats give to the one who has none" (Luke 3:11) applies here.

1 John 3:17

> But if anyone has the world's goods and sees his brother in need, yet closes his heart against him, how does God's love abide in him?

God has a huge heart for the poor and needy. Time and space doesn't permit us to drill down deeper on this, but we can see God's heart here in Proverbs 19.

Proverbs 19:17

> If you help the poor, you are lending to the Lord—and he will repay you!

Notice the connection between the Lord and giving to the poor. This is similar to what Jesus said.

Matthew 25:40

> Truly, I say to you, as you did it to one of the least of these my brothers, you did it to me.

If you read Matthew 25:31-45 you'll see that part of our final judgment is connected to how we gave to those in need. God wants to bless us so that we will bless others in need.

3. To enjoy life.

The third reason God wants us to live in abundance and be richly supplied is so that we can enjoy life unburdened from poverty and lack. The Apostle Paul had a warning to rich people, but he also tacked on something interesting.

1 Timothy 6:17

> As for the rich in this present age, charge them not to be haughty, nor to set their hopes on the uncertainty of riches, but on God, **who richly provides us with everything to enjoy.**

God provides us with everything to enjoy! God is not against this whatsoever, He just wants us to put first things first, which is following Christ (Matthew 6:33).

Deuteronomy 6:10-15

> 10 And when the Lord your God brings you into the land that he swore to your fathers, to Abraham, to Isaac, and to Jacob, to give you—with great and good cities that you did not build,
>
> 11 and houses full of all good things that you did not fill, and cisterns that you did not dig, and vineyards and olive trees that you did not plant—and when you eat and are full,

¹² then take care lest you forget the Lord, who brought you out of the land of Egypt, out of the house of slavery.

¹³ It is the Lord your God you shall fear. Him you shall serve and by his name you shall swear.

¹⁴ You shall not go after other gods, the gods of the peoples who are around you—

¹⁵ for the Lord your God in your midst is a jealous God.

We see the heart of God in this passage. God wants to bless us with abundance and nice things but commands (not suggests) that we put Him first. He is a jealous God who won't tolerate us going after our man-made idols or share His glory with anyone or anything else.

Isaiah 42:8

I will not yield my glory to another or my praise to idols. (NIV)

Yes, God wants His children to live in abundance for these three reasons as long as we put Him first.

Contentment

The balance to what was just presented on abundance is the complementary truth of living with contentment. Notice what the Apostle Paul said about this.

Philippians 4:11-13

> I have learned in whatever situation I am to be content. I know how to be brought low, and I know how to abound. In any and every circumstance, I have learned the secret of facing plenty and hunger, abundance and need. I can do all things through him who strengthens me.

Notice the word "learned," which Paul used twice here. He had to *learn* those things, which means contentment wasn't natural to him, nor is it natural to any other human being. We always want more than we have.

Proverbs 27:20

> Just as Death and Destruction are never satisfied, so human desire is never satisfied.

It's human nature to always want more, but one reason Christ came was to give us a new nature, one that is free from the love of money or things.

Hebrews 13:5

> Keep your life free from love of money, and **be content** with what you have, for he has said, "I will never leave you nor forsake you."

Wealth without intense, serious and radical commitment to following Jesus Christ sets one up to becoming a prime target. It's been that way for millennia. Listen to what James said to those who are wealthy but who didn't have full devotion or commitment to Jesus Christ.

James 5:1-3

> Come now, you rich, weep and howl for the miseries that are coming upon you. Your riches have rotted and your garments are moth-eaten. Your gold and silver have corroded, and their corrosion will be evidence against you and will eat your flesh like fire. You have laid up treasure in the last days.

The people here became prime targets because of wealth untethered to serving Christ. That is why Jesus taught that it's easier for a camel to go through the eye of a needle than for a rich person to go to heaven (Mark 10:23, 25). It's because you can't serve God and money at the same time, there's only room for one top priority.

Luke 16:13

No servant can serve two masters, for either he will hate the one and love the other, or he will be devoted to the one and despise the other. **You cannot serve God and money.**"

God wants to bless us, but it's connected to spiritual growth and putting Him first.

3 John 1:2

Dear friend, I pray that you may enjoy good health and that all may go well with you, even as your soul is getting along well. (NIV)

"All may go well with you" certainly would include adequate provision and ample besides, but it's connected to soul health. God's admonition about treasure is in Matthew 6.

Matthew 6:19-21

"Do not lay up for yourselves treasures on earth, where moth and rust[e] destroy and where thieves break in and steal, but lay up for yourselves treasures in heaven, where neither moth nor rust destroys and where thieves do not break in and steal. For where your treasure is, there your heart will be also.

"Do not lay up for yourselves treasures on earth" doesn't mean you shouldn't have abundance or a savings account. The focus is on priorities...earth or heaven, treasures or Christ? Wealth makes one a prime target if not coupled with intense commitment to following Jesus Christ.

Chapter 5

The Shield of Faith

In Chapter 2 we talked about the armor of God listed in Ephesians 6, the shield of faith being part of that ensemble.

Ephesians 6:18

> In all circumstances take up **the shield of faith**, with which you can extinguish all the flaming darts of the evil one

I believe the full impact of that verse is lost on most people. We think to ourselves, "Well, I believe in Christ, so the shield of faith is already up." I believe that's inaccurate, and I'll explain why.

We have been afforded numerous blessings and promises because we are "in" Jesus Christ, that is, we have received Jesus Christ as Lord and Savior and are actively following Him. That doesn't mean we're perfect, but we are, for the most part, putting Christ and His kingdom first place in our lives (Matthew 6:33). Most people don't comprehend all the blessings we have "in Christ."

Ephesians 2:7

That in the coming ages he might show **the
immeasurable riches of his grace** in kindness
toward us **in Christ Jesus.**

Ephesians 1:3

Blessed be the God and Father of our Lord
Jesus Christ, who has blessed us **in Christ** with
every **spiritual blessing** in the heavenly places.

"Blessed us in Christ with every spiritual
blessing" does not mean these blessings are only
experienced in heaven, not down here on earth in
this natural or practical realm. They are called
"spiritual blessings" because they are bestowed
upon us in the grace and power of the Holy Spirit.

Here is a partial list of the blessings we have in
Christ:
- Salvation (eternal life)
- Power and divine ability
- Wisdom and guidance
- Righteousness, right-standing with God
- A sound mind (intellectual and emotional wholeness)
- Health and healing
- Provision and abundance
- Protection
- Hope
- Fruit of the Spirit (peace of mind, joy, love, etc.)
- Fellowship in the Body of Christ (the church)
- Marital, family, and relational harmony

- Answered prayer
- Protection and deliverance from the enemy's attacks
- Gifts of the Spirit and divine enablements
- Purpose, meaning and mission
- Authority in the name of Jesus

These are wonderful promises and blessings that we have "in Christ." But here is the million-dollar question—do these promises and blessings AUTOMATICALLY became reality in our lives just because we're saved? We intuitively know the answer to that question...no! Our own lives demonstrate that fact. This brings us to a biblical truth which I will frame this way—we cannot "assume" God's blessings and promises, they must be grasped or received by faith. Most Christians just assume that because they are Christ-followers (notice I said *Christ-followers* not *Christ-believers*...there's a huge difference), that God's blessings will just fall on them automatically. Not true. So how do we, for lack of a better way of expressing it, "tap into" and experience these promises and blessings? And the answer to that is...praying and "appropriating" these blessings by faith.

Jesus is called "the last Adam," (1 Corinthians 15:45) because He came to restore to us everything the first Adam lost. The last enemy that is not yet defeated is physical death (1 Corinthians 15:26). Even spiritual death has been defeated and we now have a restored relationship with God through Christ. Therefore, with the exclusion of physical death, everything else has been restored back to us (health, healing, protection, provision, etc.). But these blessings don't fall on us like ripe cherries off a tree. These promises are not "realized" or experienced in our lives because we love God, go to church and are good little Christians. They must be "appropriated."

That may be a new word to you, but the verb *appropriate* means "to take possession of." It means to reach out and take something as your own...taking an action that brings something from potential to reality. For example, if you have money in your checking account and need cash, you must take an action. You can wish for money in hand all you want, but you'll never experience it until you take an action to receive it, even though it's potentially yours already. Generally, this means going to an ATM, putting in your debit card and password, selecting the amount you desire, and then taking the cash and receipt (and I've learned from experience if married to always give the receipt to your spouse or you're in trouble, but that's a different issue). The money was in your checking account (potential), but you had to take an action that tapped into that potential blessing and made it real in the here and now. This is how it works with God's promises and blessings, and the action we take is called *the prayer of faith*.

James 5:14-15

Is anyone among you sick? Let him call for the elders of the church, and let them pray over him,

111

> anointing him with oil in the name of the Lord. And **the prayer of faith** will save the one who is sick, and the Lord will raise him up.

Notice "the prayer of faith." The NIV says, "the prayer offered in faith." Prayers of petition (petition means *asking*) offered in faith are how we tap into and take possession of God-given blessings. We must ask in faith, thereby appropriating the promise and blessing of God.

James 1:5-6

> If any of you lacks wisdom, **let him ask God**, who gives generously to all without reproach, and it will be given him. But let him **ask in faith**, with no doubting.

This is true for protection, healing, financial or material provision, wisdom, guidance or any other promise of God. We're not automatically protected from accident or tragedy because we're Christians. We're not automatically healed or provided for just because we're Christians. God's Word instructs us to ask in faith for these blessings. Though these blessings come to us in Christ through God's grace, faith is still the key to appropriating those blessings. We see this principle in Romans 5.

Romans 5:2

Through him (Christ) we have also obtained **access by faith into this grace** in which we stand.

Grace is the unmerited favor of God. Encompassed within God's grace is the sum total of all of His promises and blessings that we have in Christ (notice, "through him"). And our access or doorway into all those blessings is...faith. We can wish and desire them all we want, but they are appropriated (taken possession of) by asking in faith. Mark 5 is the story of the woman with the issue of blood, what we would call hemorrhaging. She had had this condition for twelve years, and no doctor could help her. This woman pressed through the crowd to touch Jesus for she said to herself, "If I touch even his garments, I will be made well." Not "I might be," but "I will be." When she touched Jesus's garment she was immediately healed. Here's what Jesus said to her.

Mark 5:34

Daughter, **your faith has made you well**; go in peace, and be healed of your disease.

Jesus didn't say it was the healing power of God that made the woman well, although we know that it was. It's interesting that Jesus said that it was the woman's faith that made her well. Why did He put it that way? When the woman touched the hem of Jesus' garment, Jesus stopped. Verse 30 says, "Jesus realized at once that healing power had gone out from him." (NLT) Jesus felt healing power leave Him and go into the woman's body as she touched Him. The woman's faith was the copper wire that touched the power source! He said the same things to the leper who got healed.

Luke 17:19

> And he said to him, "Rise and go your way; **your faith has made you well.**"

Again, He didn't say "Rise and go your way; the power of God has made you well." Of course, it was the healing power of God that made the leper well, that's assumed. But what sparked or initiated that power to go from Jesus into the leper? Jesus said, "Your faith has made you well." It's the same thing with the blind man in Luke 18.

Luke 18:41-43

> "What do you want me to do for you?" He said, "Lord, let me recover my sight." And Jesus said to him, "Recover your sight; **your faith has made you well.**" And immediately he recovered his sight and followed him, glorifying God. And all the people, when they saw it, gave praise to God.

"Your faith has made you well." It was the blind man's faith that tapped into the healing power of

God. This is Romans 5:2, *we have access by faith into this grace.*

The action of asking in faith for protection (and other things) is how you put up the shield of faith (Ephesians 6:18), *with which you can extinguish all* (not some) *the flaming darts of the evil one.* Even if you're not a prime target, you're still a target, therefore putting up the shield of faith is a must for all believers. It's not IF the arrows will come, it's WHEN. If you don't hold off these fiery arrows with the shield of faith, those arrows will find their mark. But stay alert in prayer and put up the shield of faith using your authority in the name of Jesus. This action pushes back the enemy.

1 John 5:4

For every child of God defeats this evil world, and **we achieve this victory through our faith.**

A big part of defeating the enemy and securing victory is our faith. We must take the intentional and active step of putting up the shield of faith to extinguish all the flaming arrows of the devil.

How often must we ask in faith for God's blessings? Do you just pray once and it's good for your whole life? No. Must we ask ten times a day for protection, healing and provision? No. But I think it's a good practice to weekly go before the Lord in prayer and by faith appropriate His blessings instead of just assuming them.

James 4:2

You do not have, because you do not ask.

My hope is that you'll take away from this book some very important truths:

1. Understand that we have a very real spiritual enemy bent on destroying us.

2. Understand the enemy' tactics, such as distraction and a false sense of security.

3. Keep the enemy on our radar by staying vigilant in prayer.

4. Have an experiential knowledge of our spiritual weapons, especially the name of Jesus and the sword of the Spirit, which is the Word of God.

5. Stay closely connected to a good local church and small group of Christ-followers.

6. Do not allow wealth or secondary interests to distract us from fully devotion to Christ.

7. Put on the full armor of God.

8. Put up the shield of faith, asking the Lord in faith for protection, health/healing, provision and other blessings He has given us in Christ.

About the Author

Tom Peers has been in ministry since 1979. He grew up in Brockport, New York; attended Monroe Community College, Rochester, New York; State University of New York at Brockport, served in the United States Air Force and Air National Guard, graduated from Rhema Bible College in Broken Arrow, Oklahoma, and attended Elim Bible Institute, Lima, New York.

Tom has served as a pastor in Rochester, New York; Lake Worth, Florida; Florence, Kentucky; Cumberland, Maine and Portsmouth, New Hampshire; along with serving as Director of Operations for a Christian ministry in Phoenix, Arizona. He has also served fulltime as a certified church consultant. Tom and his wife Debby have two children, Jesse and Carissa, each with families of their own. Tom and Debby currently reside in Portland, Maine.

tompeers53@gmail.com

Books by Tom Peers

The Pastor and the Prayer
Addiction Recovery Through Living the Serenity Prayer

Lord and Savior
A Savior to be Received From – A Lord to be Obeyed

Fit, Function and Flourish
Your Place and Function in the Local Church

Is God to Blame?
Reconciling Suffering with a Good God

How to Be a Prime Target
We're All Targets – Some Make Better Targets Than Others

Mixed Nuts
Brain Droppings from a Retired Pastor

www.ingramcontent.com/pod-product-compliance
Lightning Source LLC
Chambersburg PA
CBHW032112040426
42337CB00040B/225

* 9 7 8 0 9 9 7 0 9 9 8 5 0 *